Pickleball

One Court at a Time

Building a Homegrown Program

by

Christie Borne

For the Love of the Game!
Christie Bre

Pickleball
One Court at a Time
Building a Homegrown Program

ISBN: 978-0-9828668-5-6

Copyright © 2017 Christie Borne
Library of Congress Cataloging-in-Publication Data

All rights reserved. No parts of this publication may be reproduced, stored in a retrieval system, or transmitted in any form or by any means, electronic, mechanical, photocopying, recording, or otherwise, without the prior written permission of the copyright owner.

This book is sold subject to the condition that it shall not, by way of trade or otherwise, be lent, resold, hired out, or otherwise circulated without the publisher's prior consent in any form of binding or cover other than that in which it is published and without a similar condition including this condition being imposed on the subsequent purchaser. Under no circumstances may any part of this book be photocopied for resale.

Cover photograph: **Christie Borne**
Cover Design: **Janice Massey**
Illustrations:
   Chapter icons, **Janice Massey**
   Appendix II drawings, **Emile Borne**
   Flyers: Carnival for Kids, Appendix III, IV, **Charity Hartley**
Photographs:
   Interior (unless otherwise noted), **Emile Borne**
   Back Cover, About the Author, **Cathy Wilson** (used with permission)
   sgphotos.smugmug.com
   What Others Are Saying #1, #3, **Becky Haskin**
   Group Lesson #1, **Cori McCray**

Contents

Preface	vi
About the Author	vii
Appreciation	ix
What Others Are Saying	x
Build a Foundation—Plant the Seeds	1
Capture the Players	1
First Impressions Are Important	2
Building Materials—Gather Needed Nutrients	3
Qualified Instructors and Great Volunteers	3
Pickleball Accessories—the Basics	3
Check the Calendar	4
Calendar Activities—Schedule for Abundant Growth	6
Group Lessons	6
Private and Semi-Private Lessons	7
Open Play	7
Club and Community Events	7
Demonstrations	7
How-to-Clinics	8
Game Strategy Clinics	8
Rating Clinics	8
Area Instructor Clinics	9
Facility Staff Pickleball Parties	9
Promote the Program—Spread the Fertilizer and Water	10
Word-of-Mouth Encounters	10
Local Newspaper Exposure and Subdivision Activities	10
Carnivals for Kids	11

Promotional Signs	11
School District Flyers	12
Connect with Social Media	13
Facility Program Marketing	13

Pickleball Events—Realize an Abundant Crop · 15

Demonstrations	15
DEMONSTRATION WITH A PRESENTATION	15
DEMONSTRATIONS AT A FACILITY OPEN HOUSE	16
Free Introductory Pickleball Clinics	16
Flyers and Displays	17
Holiday Mixers and Specialty Events	18
HOLIDAY MIXERS	19
OUT-OF-THE-ORDINARY MIXERS	19
FORMATS OF PLAY FOR HOLIDAY MIXERS AND EVENTS	24

Lesson Sessions—Prepare the Recipes · 26

Pickleball Plans at Facilities	27
Pickleball Plans at Independent Locations	28
Lesson Plans—Who Me?	31

Create Additional Revenue—Increase the Yield · 34

Consider the Budget—Count the Cost · 36

Best Pickleball Tips · 37

Appendices

Appendix I	– Skill Assessment Rating Sheet	39
Appendix II	– Beginner Clinics ~ Drills and Games	40
Appendix III	– Club or Facility Flyer Sample	43
Appendix IV	– Out-of-the-Ordinary Mixer Flyer Sample	44
Appendix V	– Demonstration Presentation	45

Preface

For the Love of the Game

A passion for the growth of pickleball as a sport and the love for kids and their families is just what is needed to begin a strong and successful pickleball program. Without these two perspectives, a pickleball program can easily fade away with players going to another facility or just quitting and returning to the treadmill! Who wants to do that?

Pickleball can be played anywhere, and the opportunities are there with an open mind and open eyes as one travels around a town. Many churches have family centers with high ceilings; there are pavilions, community centers, fire departments, playground parking lots, subdivisions, and one's very own cul-de-sac that could provide a new adventure to build relationships with the fun sport of pickleball. I am just one person, but the sky is the limit in finding a *place to play—"if you build it, they will come!"*

This manual will help anyone build a successful pickleball program wherever it may be located. It will also provide the tools needed to support the various planning activities throughout the year.

One must **VALUE** and **STAND BEHIND** his or her pickleball program!

This makes a person a **WINNER**, and the families introduced to the game are **WINNERS** too!

About the Author

She's the Real Dill!

As the wife of a Mission Aviation Fellowship pilot, I began rearing our four children on the island of East Kalimantan (Borneo), Indonesia. There I taught the Biblical principles of marriage to Dayak women and life issues from a Biblical perspective to teenagers. After living in the jungle for several years, our family moved to a coastal city where I was able to participate in tennis leagues with Chinese and Indonesian people, as well as other Chinese expatriates.

After 10 years on the mission field and upon returning to the States, I became a United States Professional Tennis Association (USPTA) certified wheelchair and able-bodied, tennis-teaching professional. I then began creating quality grassroots–family tennis programs in 1996 with quality programing for adults and children. One example of this is the many tennis carnivals which I conducted to captivate kids' interest for the game. I have 35 years of broad-based–tennis experience, encompassing competitive tournament play with both private and public school system instruction focusing on professionalism, teamwork, character, and sportsmanship.

I have had articles published in five issues of USPTA's ADDvantage magazine, created *Call-T'-Court Tennis* in neighborhood cul-de-sacs, and co-authored *The Opportunity to Go to the Next Level*, a tennis manual for physical education teachers. As a United States Tennis Association (USTA) School Tennis Coordinator in Colorado in 2000, I trained and supervised new clinicians preparing to conduct training for physical education teachers involved in instructing tennis and conducted 100 tennis assemblies and 7 in-service workshops.

After many years of teaching tennis in the Texas heat, I began looking for a way to move my activities indoors. One day while jogging on an overhead track above a large gym at the Cypress Creek Young Men's Christian Association (YMCA) in Houston, Texas, I envisioned the possibilities of an up-and-coming sport called *pickleball* that I had just heard about while teaching tennis in Colorado. I could imagine indoor miniature tennis courts in which I could continue instructing kids in the game of tennis while developing the sport of pickleball among the active, older adults. My knowledge and skills in tennis gave me the tools to implement a new grassroots pickleball program in the Houston area.

While retaining the vision after first hearing about pickleball in Colorado, it was still another 8 years later that I began looking into the possibilities of building an indoor program at the Cypress Creek YMCA in Houston. It was exciting to survey the opportunities available in the gym. I ran the track above the gym at different times of the day and observed that the gym remained empty most days of the week. What facility would not want to fill those hours with pickleball players? That's what I was thinking! And that is where it all began.

After all these years the vision still remains—developing each player's skills to their highest potential, motivating and challenging players through quality match play and lessons, and initiating and establishing new pickleball facilities from the ground up.

Appreciation

I thank God for the desire and creative talents He has given me to develop grassroots tennis and pickleball programs over the last 20 years. I would not have been able to create out-of-the-ordinary programs, develop a successful career, or play the sports I love so much if it weren't for Him blessing me with those gifts!

I want to thank all the families who have believed in me over the years, for the kids who loved me and gave me some most unusual drawings, and for the joy of seeing lives changed through character building while assisting players in the growth in their skills.

Emile, my husband who has the patience of Job when it comes to learning new computer skills, is also my photographer and editor. He has been a great help in the production of all my articles, flyers, and program materials, and he cheers me on into the unknown. He has shown me that faith is leaping out into the unknown—and I love the thrill of leaping.

Our children, Glory, Andrew, Grace, and Charity, began learning how to play tennis on cracked asphalt neighborhood courts with me. They helped me give tennis lessons to 5-year-olds, and as a family we staged and performed puppet shows that taught self-control, patience, and integrity while encouraging tennis interest and character development that would last a lifetime. Thanks for your prayers—and for taking up the sport of pickleball!

My sister, Janet Weston, who has always been a great support, convinced me to write an e-book and other manuals to give instructors and facilities hands-on materials to get their pickleball programs off the ground.

Many thanks to Janice Massey for her help in editing this book. Earning a bachelor's degree at the age of 35, she taught various sciences to junior high students. After teaching for 13 years, she and husband, Curtis, retired and moved to Hot Springs Village where she began a second career as a medical textbook editor. Using these skills, Janice edited and produced a newsletter for a Christian prison ministry for two years.

What Others Are Saying

"For the LOVE of the GAME. That's an understatement!"
"Pickleball was first introduced to us in the winter of 2014 in Bonita Springs, Florida. From day one, the individuals we've encountered through pickleball have been amazing—friendly, helpful, courteous, and FUN!!

We were immediately addicted to the game. We knew when we returned to Michigan that we would need to drive into Lansing or Grand Rapids to find pickleball courts. Because of this, we decided to put in a new court at our home in Sunfield, Michigan. That was the beginning for our family.

The buzz word around town seemed to be "pickleball." Many people were asking, "What is it?" In the summer of 2015 we hosted a "pickleball" party as a fund-raiser for a local project. We had our initial court, plus we taped off three more courts in the driveway. It was a huge success. Many people were able to try the game for the first time and see what it's all about. Many were ordering paddles before they left the party that night.

Living in Michigan, we obviously knew our outdoor court would have limitations! My husband decided to renovate the top of a dairy barn located on one of our farms. This court is on the second level of the barn. You enter through a door in the floor. We had the wood floor refinished, installed good lighting, insulated it, put in a furnace, and—TA-DA… we have indoor pickleball!! It is amazing how often this court is used.

We still spend our winters in Florida, but many employees, family, and friends continue to use the indoor court all winter. In fact, an online schedule was created because of its popularity!

The Haskin Girls

At the time this indoor court was being constructed, the mayor in our little local town of Sunfield was very much energized about this new, fun game. He was able to get eight courts painted at our elementary school, and two tournaments were hosted there this past year. We had many beginners but we also had some competitive individuals that drove from Lansing and Grand Rapids. A good time was had by all; and, again, some money was raised for several local nonprofit groups.

We are now in the process of working with our local high school in trying to get the "old" tennis courts converted into pickleball courts. This would be a tremendous asset to our community, being centrally located among four outlying towns. What a great way to bring the towns together! This game has totally changed how we spend a vast amount of our "free" time. We have met hundreds of new, wonderful people—all of whom are enjoying this new pastime!!"

Brian and Becky Haskin
Sunfield, Michigan

"We were wildly enthusiastic but nervous…We shouldn't have worried."

"We were members of the Cypress Creek YMCA in north Houston in 2008 when Christie started a senior pickleball program. Our program began with only 6 to 10 people. We were wildly enthusiastic but nervous that our new sport would not attract enough people to continue the program. We shouldn't have worried.

Today the program Christie began has in excess of 100 players at multiple levels, with weekly lessons at several skill levels, monthly mixers, and both morning and afternoon playing times allotted at the YMCA. The program also attracts visiting players from other Houston YMCAs and even those from out of town.

We owe the success of this program to Christie's great organizational skills, as well as the fact that all levels and ages may participate. We are excited that Christie has been instrumental in revitalizing the pickleball program in Hot Springs Village, Arkansas. We know she will have every success!"

Al and Susan Austin
Houston, Texas

"Christie Borne is a unique pickleball pioneer."

"Christie Borne is one of the few pickleball pioneers responsible for the vast and fast growth of pickleball in and around the Houston area. While still teaching tennis, Christie convinced the D. Bradley McWilliams YMCA at Cypress Creek to implement a pickleball program. She adapted her tennis lesson plans and drills to pickleball and began to recruit students. Of course, she didn't limit her enthusiasm for teaching pickleball to the Cypress Creek YMCA.

She began doing demonstrations and small clinics at other YMCAs, churches, and any place someone would let her display her new passion. Yes, she would even set up a net and hold impromptu demonstrations in parking lots.

Today, because of the efforts of Christie and a few other enthusiasts—many inspired by her—pickleball is played in YMCAs in and around the Houston area, recreation centers, and at residential tennis courts.

Houston's first USAPA-sanctioned pickleball tournaments were the result of Christie's brainstorming, planning, organizing, and recruiting. It began with a small tournament at the YMCA at Cypress Creek. Next was **The Real Dill Tournament**, again with Christie as the tournament director and driving force. That tournament now draws some top USAPA players.

Christie's pickleball accomplishments are not only limited to teaching. She is one of the top players in her age group and has medaled in numerous tournaments across the United States, as well as at the national level. She also volunteers as a referee and announcer at those tournaments.

And that's not all. For two years, Christie served on the USAPA Board of Directors and as the Chairperson for USAPA Ambassadors. Through her diligent leadership, the ambassador program grew so much that many regional directors had to appoint area directors to help 'shepherd the flock' of new ambassadors.

In July of 2013, Christie and her husband, Emile, moved to Hot Springs Village, Arkansas. Within a few months, she was elected as president of the 200–plus member Hot Springs Village Pickleball Club. She is still recruiting players, revising and creating lesson plans, teaching skills, and helping to expand another huge pickleball community.

Christie's current activity list includes work on some future pickleball publications and a possible pickleball business venture with her sister. She constantly looks for new ways to create a means to promote the sport of her passion, pickleball.

Christie has devoted many years to teaching and promoting pickleball; however, those of us who know her well understand that she always keeps her priorities prominently in order. Christie's first priority is her Lord Jesus Christ; second are her husband and wonderful family; and a distant third is pickleball and her many friends therein."

Winnie Montgomery, MA
Competed, coached, and officiated at the national level in eight different sports
Past Tournament Chair of USAPA Board of Directors
Pickleball Ambassador for 5 years

> "Pickleball is a great sport and Christie is just the teacher to bring out the best in everyone."

"From beginner to experienced players, Christie has the technique and knowledge to improve anyone's game. She is the best!"
George Dodge
Houston, Texas

> "I was one of Christie's original pickleball students at our YMCA in Houston, Texas."

"We continued our classes several years, and never once was she unprepared with her written drills, time schedule, and purpose for each. She was an active recruiter for the game and a constant ambassador for pickleball. As a fellow teacher, I have great respect for her teaching, as well as respect for the integration of her Christian values into her teaching as she leads by example influenced by those values."
Ann Redman, Cypress Creek YMCA Pickleball Instructor
Houston, Texas

> "After only a few months of playing, we were competing in tournaments, winning our share of medals, and most importantly, having fun!"

"I first heard about pickleball in October of 2008. I was a member of the Cypress Creek YMCA when Christie asked if I would be interested in playing a racket sport. I agreed but explained that I had never played any racket games. The program started with six of us in the gym where Christie was demonstrating pickleball and then had us participate by hitting the ball across the net. I was hooked from the start! Six of us signed up for lessons. Christie developed a program of lessons, as well as open play time, and our skill level improved greatly. The pickleball program began by Christie at the Cypress Creek YMCA started with only six players on one court. It now has increased to 5 courts with over 100 players and is still growing."
Joe Parnell, 86 years old
Houston, Texas

Build a Foundation—Plant the Seeds

To begin building the foundation for pickleball activities, more than one possible location should be considered. Check to see what is available in the surrounding area. Are there unused tennis courts in a recreation park, a community center gym not being used, or a school district needing an after-school program? Wherever it is, this is the first step to creating a viable program.

Some of the things to look for are: appropriate lighting, hours of access, storage space for balls, nets, and equipment, and a probable client base. Is this a favorite place for families? Is there frequent turnout? And what expected costs are there for setting up a facility pickleball program?

Capture the Players

What types of groups would one want to go after? At the beginning of the adventure in 2008, my program at the YMCA was created for active older adults. They had very few vigorous activities for people between the ages of 60 to 80, and so pickleball caught on quickly and grew from 6 players on one court to 125 players and 5 courts. However, as the pickleball program grew, we began to pursue younger players, for it was no longer a program just for active older adults.

A summer program for teenagers during the day or a nighttime pickleball for kids should definitely be considered. Many men under 50 years of age have a need to sweat; Saturday mornings or evenings would be a great time for them.

First Impressions are Important

One should prepare a well-written resume with stated objectives, a list of latest jobs, any publications to which articles have been submitted and published, and a description of education and degrees earned. Bullet points should be kept short and to the point. The reader should be left with enough information about personal character, work ethic, and skills so it can be determined if this is the candidate to promote their pickleball program. Any phrases such as "I did this" or "I am good at this," should be avoided. An enthusiastic candidate will discover the names of directors of recreation or the facility managers at several locations and set up appointments to present the qualifications, passion, and vision needed for a successful pickleball program. The serious candidate will dress as a professional, rather than someone who just finished jogging 10 miles. It really does make a difference! *Don't you think?*

Face to Face—be prepared with the facts about pickleball because many facilities have never heard of the sport before. Here is a list of relevant facts:

- Pickleball is the fastest growing sport in America—it is a lifetime sport unlike soccer, basketball, or football.
- It appeals to athletes, as well as to those who have never played a racquet sport before.
- It is better to be involved in a sport than jogging on a treadmill and staring at a television set.
- It is interactive in nature and a place where new friendships can be formed.
- It creates new profits for any YMCA or facility because it builds memberships and increases the utilization of equipment.

Building Materials—Gather Needed Nutrients

Qualified Instructors and Great Volunteers

Whether building a house or a model airplane, one needs the right materials for a successful structure. The total cost should be counted before beginning any new project. Even giving a great first demonstration but having no one to continue promoting it, may cause the program to fold.

After providing pickleball demonstrations to churches and YMCAs in the Houston area only to see the death of those pickleball plans, we realized that a core group of players who can run with the program or good instructors with good volunteers is crucial. It's best not to depend upon the employees of the facility unless they have the same kind of fervor for the game as the planners.

Pickleball Accessories—the Basics

- Lesson plans for instructors of beginners through advanced should be provided.
- Between 50 to 100 balls if instructors leading drills will be present.
- A diagram of court dimensions should be provided.

- Floor tape, sidewalk chalk or outdoor tape can be found at paint stores, Lowe's, or physical education equipment stores.
- Inexpensive composite paddles (lighter than wood) are usually bought by the facility—wood paddles are too heavy and may just sit in storage.
- Balls—the color of indoor balls to be determined by the color of the floors (contrasting colors are most visible) and whether or not the floors are tile, cement, or wood. Outdoor balls come in a variety of colors as well.
- Rules—the USA Pickleball Association (USAPA) is a great resource. The *Official USAPA-IFP Tournament Rule Book* can be purchased at the USAPA website (*http://www.usapa.org/ifp-official-rules/*); or the *International Federation of Pickleball Official Tournament Rule Book* may be downloaded and printed from the site in PDF format.)
- USAPA Nets—Good nets are important! At first we bought the cheap nets with bases that may be filled with sand. In order to get the regulation height for match play, we used bungee cords attached to folding chairs on either end of the court that had 20-pound weights attached on the seats. Not good! Very ingenious though! Order the nets from USAPA or from other companies that offer quality nets.
- Policies on inappropriate language, no-shows for scheduled lessons, sign-up instructions, and waivers. This information should be handed out at the beginning of the program, especially if doing one's own startup program.

Check the Calendar

Many YMCAs and community centers organize their programs around a school district's holiday and sports schedule in order to attract more kids and adults throughout the week. For instance, our tennis program was six weeks long and began at 5:30 p.m. so that parents could make sure their kids were on time for lessons. In the summer, tennis was moved to 7:00 p.m. Our adult pickleball *Open Play* was not affected except during the holidays when the kids took over the gym.

Building closures will also affect the planning of events and programs so be sure to check the facility calendar. If attempting to attract adults who often fill half the gym as Zumba dancers, then don't schedule pickleball at the same time on the other half of the gym. This will allow the Zumba dancers (or whatever activity is being done) the opportunity to participate in a new sport scheduled at a different time. This will also diminish any negative feelings or attitudes that could affect any pickleball activity plans.

Calendar Activities—Schedule for Abundant Growth

Group Lessons

A qualified volunteer or paid instructor who is skilled at teaching group or private lessons will cause the pickleball program to grow as players see their own progress. Once an instructor begins with a group for lessons, he or she needs to stick with them, close registration, and add no new players until the series is finished.

If a new player is added to an existing group, then the instructor may have to begin teaching the very skills taught to the group weeks earlier. This can seriously affect the motivation of those in the existing group to stay with this instructor. A good instructor should limit the instructor-player ratio so that players are not standing too much of the time rather than drilling. Players paying for lessons are more regular in attendance as they are spending money to develop skills. The instructor can build lessons around a particular stroke in order to develop consistency and confidence in the player. If Betty Sue decides to go out for lunch rather than develop her skills, then the facility and the instructor are still being paid.

Private and Semi-Private Lessons

Private and semi-private lessons can be profitable for the facility, as well as the instructor and should be scheduled according to the needs of the player and of instructor availability. (Instructors who are paid to teach on neighborhood courts or at local parks and recreation facilities need to understand requirements of the governing authority for liability insurance before conducting lessons. The company I use is the K&K Insurance Group, Inc. (*http://www.KandKinsurance.com*).

Open Play

If beginning with a small group of players, then it may be unnecessary to divide open play according to skill groups. However, if beginning with large groups with differing skill levels, then separate days, times, or court assignments should be considered. (It would not be good to lose top players and memberships because playing opportunities are not provided for them.) Lower skill-level players could have their own courts to be able to compete against peers and improve the consistency of their shots. In addition, lessons will quickly increase their skill level rather than just competition alone. A good rule of thumb is to provide one hour of skilled format and another hour divided into mixed-skill courts.

Club and Community Events

Events for families, women, men, children, or adults may be scheduled in a club or in another community facility. Creative "thinking outside the box" will attract many. Adding food to any event guarantees a good social time as well.

Demonstrations

Many YMCAs have events such as *Family Night, Healthy Kids Day, Wear Pink for Breast Cancer Month,* or other opportunities that provide a venue for free demonstrations. Portable nets can be set up in the parking lot, under a pavilion, in the racquetball court, or in the foyer of a facility or gym.

How-to-Clinics

How-to-clinics are special events that challenge players to learn something new or to help them work on perfecting a skill they may already have. Some suggestions for these clinics are:
- Lobs and Lob Recovery
- Hitting an Effective Soft/Slow Paced Ball
- Add Spin to Your Serve
- Footloose & Fancy Free Footwork

Game Strategy Clinics

Skill-oriented clinics such as the following could be held:
- Moving as a Team
- Which Doubles' Partner Takes Which Shot
- Opening Gaps for a Winner
- Partner Stacking

Rating Clinics

Rating clinics involve at least two or three qualified instructors or players with knowledge of the game and who have played in tournaments. These should be asked in advance to conduct the rating clinics in time for optimal planning. Players play in a doubles format according to their self-rating. Players receive three evaluations which would be based upon the level they play as an individual. A skill sheet example is available in Appendix I at the back of the book and all skill sheets may be found at the USAPA website *(http://www.usapa.org/skill-assessment-sheets/)*.

Area Instructor Clinics

A three-hour clinic for new instructors could be organized to develop skills of teaching, laying lines, setting up drills, and creating lesson plans. (Then get together for a sandwich or something!) I held such a clinic in Houston and invited all employees from local YMCAs who were interested in beginning a program. Our clinic was quite successful.

Facility Staff Pickleball Parties

A quarterly event for the staff of a facility could be established so they may become acquainted with pickleball. The staff needs to be knowledgeable about the game and be able to promote pickleball when new members inquire about the latest activities. Order in pizza or go out for it together!

Promote the Program—Spread the Fertilizer and Water

Word-of-Mouth Encounters

Sharing pickleball activities by word of mouth is one of the best ways of attracting new players. My first tennis program began on the cracked asphalt courts in my neighborhood in Ft. Worth, Texas. Because I had a real passion both for tennis and for the desire to see character built into kids' lives, I volunteered to teach a character-building tennis class for 5 and 6 year olds. My children and I put on puppet shows using a quilt hung over the tennis net for a stage. I then taught tennis skills while implementing character building at the same time. As tales of the fun, new tennis activities were shared by word of mouth from the kids to the parents, one group of six ladies and another group of five children from our church was started.

Local Newspaper Exposure and Subdivision Activities

Local advertising, even in small newspapers or community bulletin boards, is a great asset for attracting attention to a new pickleball program. After moving to Colorado in 1996, I created my own tennis program on little-used courts. I learned to take advantage of the local subdivision newspaper. Each group of kids formed was given a name—the *Future Stars*, the *Shinning Stars*, and the *Shooting Stars*. I designed eye-catching flyers describing the programs and was given permission by the school district to hand these out in each class of the elementary school which was across the street from the courts. As people drove by the courts and saw the kids taking lessons, they became curious, discovered the program, and began to sign up for classes. I suddenly had a full teaching schedule.

Carnivals for Kids

During my time teaching tennis, I organized a tennis carnival to attract players during a day of activities sponsored by my subdivision. I purchased tennis prizes such as ball banks, pens, key chains (may be ordered through a tennis products distributing company) and these were awarded as prizes. Activities called *Beat the Pro and Turkey Shoot* were set up as "courts." (I bought big turkey posters from a school supply company, attached them to a one-quarter inch x 2 ft. piece of plywood, and then hung them on the fence with tie wraps.) Kids were challenged to drop-hit forehand ground strokes and kill a turkey! A little "hip" music added and everyone was moving to the beat of the ball! After the carnival, the kids were really pumped about tennis. This same scenario could be used for a pickleball carnival. So find some pickleball giveaways, put on some music, and develop some fun pickleball games for the kids.

> **HOT SPRINGS VILLAGE PICKLEBALL KIDS CARNIVAL**
>
> "*Come One! Come All! Step right up and have a ball!*"   Ages 5-8
>
> ◆◆◆◆◆◆◆◆◆◆◆◆◆◆◆◆◆◆◆◆
> **PICKLEBALL GAMES:**
>
> GAUNTLET   HOOLA
> DOUBLE TROUBLE HOOP HOPS
> EAR MUFFS   TIGHT WIRE
> picklebowl golf   Anything Goes
>
> • PRIZES AND CANDY •
> ◆◆◆◆◆◆◆◆◆◆◆◆◆◆◆◆◆◆◆◆
> SEPTEMBER 3, 2017   6:00 - 7:30 PM
> HOT SPRINGS VILLAGE, ARKANSAS

Promotional Signs

Purchased signs displaying relevant pickleball information placed in strategic locations may also help gain attention for the program. **A word of caution:** Be sure to check any homeowner association

(HOA) rules regarding sign placement. One year I made the mistake of not inquiring beforehand of the HOA policies in a particular subdivision. I purchased 50 signs that probably cost me $100. I placed them at key corners and on the busiest streets of the subdivision. A day later I received a call from the HOA saying that the signs had been removed because they were illegal in that particular neighborhood (fortunately, I was later able to recover them from their office). I then just used one of the 50 to put in my own front yard and placed a few others in front of the tennis building to promote my *Survive the Heat Summer Tennis Camps*. The rest of the signs—well, you know the story!

Those who build their own programs without the financial support of a local YMCA, community center, or parks and recreation facility, may need to "think outside the box" to announce a new pickleball adventure. This may also require spending one's own money to do so. As an example, I created flyers which I distributed at the Walmart parking lot into open car windows. I also posted the flyers on structures in local tennis court parking lots where people could see them easily. Windshield wipers can secure a flyer until the owner has a chance to retrieve and read it!

School District Flyers

Having access to public or even private schools greatly helps in distributing pickleball flyers and, thus, gaining participants. In 2003 I was hired as a children's tennis pro at Raveneaux Country Club in Houston, Texas. This was my first real tennis job working for a facility. Since the club's 16 courts were also available to the school district for tournaments and practices, I was allowed to place flyers in all the schools. This meant that I needed to create the flyer, have thousands of them printed, and then deliver them to each school.

Although I spent many hours creating the flyer, packaging them, and hours on the road delivering them, it all paid off with an expansion of the children's programs. It also added much-needed revenue for the facility. I was an unknown tennis-teaching pro at the time, but the work done and time spent was well worth gaining a full schedule of teaching children's tennis.

Connect with Social Media

The most common social media websites online are Facebook, Twitter, Pinterest, LinkedIn, and Instagram. Facebook is the most popular and a great place to promote a new pickleball program. It can be used to build a community of people who might be interested in the new program. It is a place to expose your program to potential new players and to inform those who already play that a new venue has been created. It is relatively easy to set up and post pictures of the facility where the activities are to be held and to announce upcoming events with posted flyers (as images). Clinic information regarding match times, dates of play, lessons, and prices can be posted, as well as information regarding canceling an event or lessons. Tournaments, contests, and free coupons can also be posted to create excitement about the new lifetime sport.

Using several people as administers to create a unique Facebook page is a plus. This allows for more input and is less of a burden for one person to maintain. The *Wall* tells about the Facebook page. The *News Feed* is what is posted on the status icon that goes to all those on a list of followers or "friends." I did not use Facebook to build my tennis and pickleball programs, but in reality, that is what is popular in today's world.

Facility Program Marketing

Better than marketing a new pickleball program on a personal level (and with one's personal resources and money), having a facility to do so is a much better choice. In 2008 I created my own pickleball job at the Cypress Creek YMCA in Houston. It was a relief to know that they would be doing the promoting using their own flyers and sending the information to all of the schools and neighborhoods in the area. This was amazing because it allowed me to focus more on gathering information about pickleball and writing lesson plans rather than on advertising it. Remember, I had only heard of the sport, had never actually played it, and didn't have a clue about the rules.

After some research, I decided the first thing to do was to find a venue to demonstrate pickleball. I did so during an active older adult open house in the fall of 2008, with plans of beginning 6 weeks of lessons to follow that event. I invited a few people I had never met but who played pickleball and asked them to direct the event. It was fun and crazy to try and hit a plastic ball with a small paddle half the size of a tennis racquet; but it was a great time and also very informative.

Pickleball Events—Realize An Abundant Crop

Demonstrations

DEMONSTRATION WITH A PRESENTATION

Demonstrations that attract a crowd of people are a great way to promote a program for pickleball. These should be advertised to be held at a designated time and place. A one- to two-hour block of time allows some fun with the crowd. Getting many active in some short drills and actually playing the game can be very entertaining.
- Setting a date on the calendar for the demonstration at least a month ahead is the first priority.
- Promoting the event through media, flyers, and by the using display tables in strategic locations is next.
- Making a checklist of equipment is definitely needed. These include items such as paddles, balls, sign-in sheets, and armband identifiers for the first server of each team, announcement of playing times, free lesson coupons, and flyers that include times for lessons, mixers, and open-play hours.
- Handing out quirky prizes is always a good icebreaker.
- Preparing an introduction and even using a "script" is necessary. The spokesperson needs to be fun and informative, as well as concise. Be aware of the time (don't drone on) and the facial expressions (bored or paying attention) of the listeners. The speaker needs to just "win the day"!
- Including as many players as possible on the court during the participation phase of the demonstration will guarantee a winning time (pardon the pun!) for all.
- Preparing and organizing the planned demonstration is essential to success. Appendix V contains a great Demonstration/Presentation sample.

It would be great if two or more players, invited several weeks before a demonstration, could assist in demonstrating the game.

As the spokesperson (or yourself) talks to the crowd, these assistants can easily demonstrate the strokes for pickleball. Purchasing a lapel microphone or using one from the facility ensures that one can be heard over the bouncing ball. The sound equipment, or any batteries used in equipment, should be checked for any problems the day before the event. On the day of the event, paddles could be placed near the net (or possibly in a plastic bucket) to keep them from getting scattered on the floor. Equipment such as cones, flyers, paddles, prizes, or whatever is needed, should be carried in a duffel bag that can be easily moved from one court to the other. (I carry a frying pan to demonstrate how easy it is to hit volleys without even using a paddle—but that is just me!)

Demonstrations at a Facility Open House

Another type of demonstration is a facility open house. The facility's gym or racquetball court should be reserved ahead of time to make sure the demonstration will be on the calendar of events. On the day of the demonstration, while someone is manning a pickleball display table in the foyer of a facility, another volunteer can direct interested players to the gym, racquetball court, or parking lot where the event is taking place. Another volunteer or the pickleball instructor should be on the court waiting to introduce newly interested people to the sport. A handful of players usually join the fun, and it doesn't take long for the crowd on the court to grow. The instructor or volunteer should be prepared to hit a few balls with players so they can get the feel and the thrill of the game. Close to the ending time for the demonstration, information for pickleball clinics and flyers with other pickleball activities could be handed out with the hope that the demonstration participants will return as real players.

Free Introductory Pickleball Clinics

A free introductory pickleball demonstration could be set up every few weeks. I like to encourage interested players to sign up before a clinic with a minimum of four players. The maximum number of players would depend upon how many instructors are available to help conduct the demonstration and introduction to the game. At one of my introductory clinics, I had two instructors on one court conducting drills together. After a short break they divided the players onto two courts to play the game. My free introductory clinic was approximately 1 ½ hours long and incorporated the following lesson plan:

Introductory Plan:
- Introduction and welcome
- History of pickleball
- Membership and information about the USAPA
- Facility events
- Paddle vendors and types of paddles
- Handouts that include a list of simple rules, membership forms, and vendor information
- Warm-up: stretching and jogging
- Volley, ground stroke, and service drills
- Explanation of the pickleball rules (from the handout), court etiquette, and the court lines
- Play the game

Other teachers disagree that drills are necessary, but I believe players who can execute a variety of shots when they play the actual game (the balls going back and forth over the net), are more capable than those who just serve and return (if even that!).

Flyers and Displays

The facility staff should be prepared to give a lively description of pickleball and have the pickleball flyers in view of people coming into the facility. There is nothing worse than a staff that has no idea what pickleball is or even know if it exists at the facility. Front desk staff should begin promoting the game before potential clients are even seen. (A flyer could show pictures of the paddles and balls and be given out to the staff.)

Sign-up sheets with name, email, and cell phone number should be prepared for interested players. These should be available and visible on a display table. The display table should be set up when a majority of the targeted population would be coming into the facility.

It should include:
- USAPA promotional DVD (available at *www.USAPA.org*) and a laptop computer
- Flyers that contain information about group lessons—cost, days, weeks, times, mixers, clinics, and open gym times
- Balls and several paddles
- Medals, pictures, and any other objects that would attract attention to the display table

Racquetball players involved in a game at the facility might be persuaded to try using a pickleball paddle and ball inside the racquetball court.

A fun way to attract attention is to appear in a paper chef's hat, holding a paddle covered with tin foil, and offering pickles on a skewer to all who walk by. Attention-grabbing phrases such as "Try pickleball—you will really *relish* this new sport"; or "Pickleball is a really *sweet* sport"; or "*Jar* yourself out of your normal routine—pickleball is just the sport for you." (One needs to be an entertainer using an excited voice. Someone who just stands behind a table will not get much attention!)

Carrying a paddle and a ball into a weight room where people are jogging on treadmills or sitting behind exercise machines is a different way to publicize pickleball activities. Along with telling them about the game of pickleball, handing them a free *One-Time Group Lesson Coupon* (to be presented on the day and time of the clinic) is a great attention-getter.

Holiday Mixers and Specialty Events

Scheduling pickleball mixers around holidays is easy because they already have a holiday theme. These mixers can be very simple or quite involved and entertaining. It depends on the time one has to create the event, which can be a challenge around the holidays. Deciding to invite pickleball players from other facilities, having just an in-house pickleball event, or making it a *bring-a-friend* event is up to the one sponsoring the mixer. It is also important to decide on the format of play in planning the event. One of the things I loved about my job as a self-employed tennis and pickleball director was to be able to create the activities that I wanted, have it approved by a facility, and then run with it!

Holiday Mixers

Valentine's Day: Sweet Spot Mixed Couples—for the LOVE of the GAME. Men may bring a carnation for their partner or, better yet, the mixer director could provide the men with red carnations.

St. Patrick's Day: Fling into Spring—Wear Green. The theme is green!

Easter: IHOP to Pickleball. All players meet for breakfast at an IHOP restaurant after match play; or players bring an assortment of rolls or casseroles for a nice time of fellowship and brunch.

Cinco de Mayo: Let's Fiesta! No time for Siesta! (Electricity is needed for this mixer to keep food heated, as well as a box of small Frito bags purchased from Sam's or Costco.) During breaks in matches, players make tacos-on-the-run with their favorite fixings dumped into the Frito bag. They can walk around visiting with other players while enjoying an unusual taco in a bag.

Father's Day: Two Old Goats (65 to 85)—Men's Doubles. Pickleball ladies will volunteer to be the referees for every match. They honor the men by providing towels or ice cold drinks. The idea, girls, is to serve the men!

Thanksgiving: Turkey Shoot-Out—A Fowl Event for Couples. Have fun and just *wing* it!

Christmas: The Twelve Days of Christmas Cookie Exchange.

Out-of-the-Ordinary Mixers

Most of my creative ideas came from looking at billboards, television commercials, or product branding at the grocery store. Many tennis professionals and clubs also have ideas which will work as well. However, to make a pickleball program fun and a little quirky, one needs to "let the creative juices flow." Looking at the surroundings of a facility to find what could be used to create an event—a pavilion, picnic tables, barbecue grills, a beach, sand, a track above the gym, a cul-de-sac, or a high volley ball net—may result in new, fresh ideas.

> **Vayamos de Fiesta**
>
> The salsa is HOT,
> the sweat will flow.
> It's Vayamos de Fiesta,
> Ya know!
>
> DETAILS:
> Date: Friday May 13
> Time: 3:00 – 6:00 pm
> Where: Outdoor courts on Desoto Blvd
> Format: Open play – choose a court, find someone you don't know or play with friends
> HSV Club Members Only
>
> **T.O.T.R (Tacos On The Run) Fiesta**
>
> - Taco/salad, Appetizers, Desserts
> - BYOBeverage & BYOSeating
> - Please bring appetizers like chips, salsa, guac, veggies, dips etc.
> - Bring food to the tent near the Rec Building
>
> SIGN UP here:
> http://www.signupgenius.com/go/20f0f48aeab23a4f49-vayamos
>
> **Friday**

The following suggested events were created for different skill levels, but could be used for a variety of skills.

Dink n' Sync: Session I

Dink Games: Players will play dink games to 11 points and win by 1 point. All players will begin behind the non-volley line. Any ball landing outside the non-volley zone is a fault. Serving will be crosscourt as usual; however, on the serve, the centerline will have to be imagined. The double-bounce rule still applies on the return of serve.

Dink n' Sync: Session II

Real Pickleball Games: Players will play to 11 points and win by 1 point. Players are encouraged to play regular pickleball but practice the dink game and stay in sync!

Pepperoni Pickleball: Players play a set number of matches and then meet at the local pizza parlor for lunch or dinner. (Give the pizza parlor a "heads up" so they have extra help if 50 players walk through the door!)

Tailgating n' Pickleball: Any parking lot will do for a tailgate party after a day of pickleball. Only those vehicles that have tailgates will be used to provide a place for appetizers, desserts, and sandwiches. Players are encouraged to bring their own lawn chairs. Everyone will have a great time selecting foods from the tailgates of different vehicles.

It may be necessary to check with the fire department about their policies on gatherings, as well as the facility about the use of their parking lot before making the preparations for the event.

Strut Your Stuff—New Turkeys to Pickleball: Players will play to 11 points and win by 1 point. Each match will have a referee who will call the score, non-volley faults, and service foot faults. A player may ask a referee *only* three questions.
1. A player will be able to contest a line call by requesting a referee decision. If the referee saw the ball, then his decision will be final.
2. A player may ask the referee if he or she is in the correct position.
3. A player may ask the referee if he or she is the correct server or the receiver.

Because referees are used at all USAPA-sanctioned tournaments for every match, they should be used in any pickleball games to ensure the use of proper rules. This takes the pressure off the players so they are able to concentrate on the game. It also would be beneficial to use the USAPA score sheets printed from the *www.USAPA.org* website.

Blind Dates: Women are blindfolded and players are divided into skill sections: 2.5 to 3.0; 3.5; or 4.0 to 4.5. An equal number of men and women are needed for each skill category. A set of rules should be created that the women must follow in order to choose their partner.

Suggested rules could be:
- Women may not touch a man between his shoulders and knees.
- Men may not speak or touch the woman attempting to check out a possible partner.
- Women may touch a partner's hair (if he has any), his glasses, his hands, or his shoes. (The shape of a hat, straight, curly, or no hair, or tall or short may be a giveaway.)
- After the woman has chosen the male partner, she may remove the blindfold and will stay with her partner the rest of the evening.

Battle of the Sexes: Handicap Doubles. The play activity may involve several arrangements—two women versus one man, or two women against two men. Men play with their non-dominate hand and must either carry or wear one of the items listed below. (This should be tested first with a few players before announcing it as an event.) A fun twist to this activity is to have players (or others watching) place bets on the competitors with winnings going to the facility. It might be beneficial to visit a resale shop for some of the following items:
- Bag of 10-roll count toilet paper (to be carried under the arm)
- Big bag of *Depends* (carried under the arm)
- Stuffed toy teddy bear
- Sling for a broken arm
- Football or bicycle helmet

- Football shoulder pads
- Cooler (similar to a quart-drink size)
- Scarf to be worn around the neck while carrying a large ladies handbag in his non-dominant hand

Swing to the Beat: Pickleball and Line Dancing. During a halftime break at the event have fun line dancing. Ladies and "gents" wear their cowgirl and cowboy hats, bring their boots, and kick up their heels! Someone who teaches line dancing could be invited to give lessons. A boom box or other portable music player should be on hand, as well as some good dancing songs such as *Prop Me Up Beside the Jukebox* by Joe Diffie. (It'll be a hoot!)

Cinderella Shoe-In: (If the shoe fits—wear it—and play with a prince.) This event has had limited appeal in past efforts. It requires an equal number of men and women. In some activities, I divided the players into 2.5 and 3.0 skill-level groups because we wanted the most players of each skill playing together.

Each female participant on the registration list brings a "representative" identifiable shoe at whatever time is specified. A fall party with a hot dog roast or a cocktail party the night before is a good way to kick-start the fun. The representative shoes of the women in the 2.5 skill group go in a black plastic bag while the shoes of the 3.0 skill group go into another black bag. The representative shoe could be a combat boot, flip-flop, ski boot, bedroom slipper, roller skate, high-heel, or any other type of footwear. While socializing and eating a light lunch, each man of the 2.5 and 3.0 skill groups will draw a shoe from the same skill-level sack. The owner of the chosen shoe will then partner with that player for the Round Robin Couples event. Once partners are found (and the shoe fitted to the owner), match play will begin.

Cross-Eyed Doubles: This event is played in a Round-Robin format with two balls in play at the same time.
- Games can be played to an 11-point limit, a 15-point limit, or a 21-point limit with a win by 1 point.
- Points are scored on all rallies by either team.
- This out-of-the-ordinary game consists of two players on the serving team positioned at one baseline and two players on the receiving team positioned at the other baseline.
- Whichever team is designated as the serving team will begin the play by exclaiming "Go." Both serving team players attempt to serve at the same time into the correct service squares.
- If the serving team wins 1 point and the receiving team wins 1 point from the same rally, then the serving team continues to serve.
- As the serving team continues to win, they will alternate service courts after every serve so that the serving team is not always serving to the same receiver.
- The serving team must honor the two-bounce rule.

- The receiving team must put the ball into play by returning it crosscourt.
- After returning the ball crosscourt, any player may hit either ball.
- Both balls are "point balls."
- One point can be won on each ball by either team.
- If the serving team loses by losing both balls in the same rally, then the receiving team becomes the serving team for the next points.

Charitable Events: Combining pickleball activities with charitable organizations' events can be beneficial for both. The organization receives the donations; the pickleball program receives recognition. Everyone has a great time, as well as feeling good about helping the organization. A schedule of these events is usually found in the local newspaper or from the Chamber of Commerce. Suggested pickleball activities at these events are:
- **Pickled Pink** for Breast Cancer Month
- **Amateur-Facility Players** for Teen Challenge
- **Serve Up a Winner** for American Heart Association, Heart to Heart Month
- **Strut Your Mutt** for dog shelters
- **Inspired Pickleball** for Fellowship of Christian Athletes

FORMATS OF PLAY FOR HOLIDAY MIXERS AND EVENTS

Open Play: When players check in at the event table, they will receive a name tag containing a number from one to four. Before a game begins, players connect to compare name tag numbers to ensure there are four different numbered players on the court. Upon completing a round of pickleball, each player must find four different players for the next match and repeat this step until all have played. This will encourage players to play with many different people throughout the event.

Round-Robin Play: Before the event, players' names are listed on a large white board for all players to see. Each player's name has a sequential number written beside it. The Round-Robin format can be used for either a team match event or for individuals playing with a different player each round. Players can play to an 11-point limit and win by 2 points. After the first court finishes, calling "rally scoring" will ensure that the rest of the games will be completed sooner. Rally scoring means *a point is scored on each rally rather than by the serving team only.*

Methods for assigning partners in Round-Robin play are:

- **Bucket Ball:** Sequential numbers are written on half as many balls as there are players; balls are then placed in a bucket. The same sequential numbers are then written on the other half of the balls; these balls are placed in another bucket. Players pick a ball from the buckets until all balls are gone. Players are matched by number for partners—one to one, two to two, three to three, four to four. After players return the balls to their respective buckets, their names and their partners' names are listed with matching numbers on a whiteboard.

- **Lotto or "Spin for a Partner":** For this game, a roulette or Bingo wheel is needed. It could be borrowed from a facility—such as a local Catholic church—or possibly rented. All players receive a number. Half the players spin the wheel, and the number on which the spinner lands is the players' partner; or, if it is a mixed couples' event, the men spin for a female partner. Players can either play the entire event together or split up the hours of play into another spin-for-a-partner!

Lesson Sessions—Prepare The Recipes

After all the introductions, demonstrations, advertisements, and exposure to pickleball in the community, it is time for actual lessons. Several decisions may need to be made beforehand. First, will the lessons be taught at a facility with areas that may be designated for pickleball activities, in a subdivision on plain asphalt that would require some involvement from volunteers or approval by an HOA to become usable, or in another type of venue? Next, how many players have signed up for lessons, how many will be in each group, what age groups will be involved, and who will teach each group?

If teaching lessons at a facility or club, then fees for lessons, the scheduling of lessons, and facility rules will need to be considered. If lessons will be taught on a "homegrown" court (in a subdivision), questions might include: how the court will be constructed; what permissions or rules are needed from the HOA; what scheduling times will be appropriate to decrease any conflicts between students and those living in the neighborhood; amount of fees charged for lessons (may be reduced compared to a facility); and the ease or difficulty of equipment transfer on and off the court. If a community tennis court is used, items to consider are permission from the local government, conflicts in scheduling times so as not to be in conflict with tennis players, any court fees, and fees for pickleball lessons given.

Two important ingredients are absolutely necessary to begin and further develop a pickleball program—a core group of people that play the game with exuberance that spills over into the lives of people they meet and a qualified teacher to give lessons.

A qualified teacher will have certain personal supplies on hand when giving lessons. A very important part of the pickleball game is—of course—the ball! Purchasing 75 to 100 balls is a good starting supply to have on hand. Another consideration before purchasing balls is whether one will be teaching indoors or outdoors (purchasing a mix of indoor and outdoor balls is recommended). The appropriate type of ball should be used for the surface being played upon. Because so many balls will be used in giving lessons, a ball container is important. (I own Hoag tennis ball hoppers which are very sturdy and hold about 60 balls each. I have owned these for more than 10 years. They stand and fold up quite easily.)

Also needed are six to eight simple composite or lightweight wooden paddles that are easy to grip and can be found online. Paddle vendors in the local area might be persuaded to give a new teacher a 10% discount rather than he or she having to pay full price.

Most importantly, for an effective beginning and animated growth, the instructor needs to have considerable energy, to be an entertainer of sorts, to enjoy interactive drills and games, and to be prepared before each lesson.

Pickleball Plans at Facilities

The first step in beginning a pickleball program using a facility such as a YMCA or club is the approach. Gaining a meeting with a director will provide pertinent information regarding the game of pickleball and its growth, as well as introduce a capable instructor. A positive outcome occurs if the instructor is hired by the facility to develop the program. The next step is becoming familiar with the facility's policies and procedures. The rate for players' lessons is usually set by the management. Players will typically pay for the lessons when they register at the front desk. After all arrangements have been made, the prepared instructor will:

- Prepare lesson plans several months in advance before actually beginning to teach. This will allow the instructor time to plan a definite strategy for organizing the program and the lessons. It also allows time to produce flyers to distribute to players and students regarding clinic dates or other information.
- Offer six one-hour group lessons for a particular group of players.
- Attend open play to view the skills of the players before asking them to join a skill group.
- Schedule several beginner clinics if it is obvious all the players have never held a paddle.

- After six weeks, evaluate the groups. Each player should be evaluated and either advanced to another group with similar skills or be asked to take another session at that particular skill level. A calm, professional tone should be used when speaking to the players concerning their skills. It has been my experience that players will usually listen to the professional instructor rather than become belligerent just to advance their own skill rating.
- Separate group lessons into beginner, intermediate, and advanced skill levels. If different skill-level players are in one group, then developing the skills of the intermediate group will suffer as more time will be spent teaching a beginner. A recommendation from the instructor should be given before the player can move to another skill group.
- Set group size, if possible. Four to six players in a group is the best size for teaching. If the group has eight players, then the balls need to be fast-fed during drills because players would rather be moving than standing. Five players in the group is an awkward number, but it can be done if the instructor plans ahead on how to rotate players in and out for game situations. A group of six players allows the instructor to set up game-type situations during the lessons so players may put into real play what they have just been taught.
- Use the facility's copy machine for handouts regarding information about pickleball rules and activities. Flyers such as *Simple Rules*, *Strategies for Doubles Teams*, *Skill Ratings*, or any other information can help someone less skilled become a better player. Many of these suggested handouts can be found online.

Pickleball Plans at Independent Locations

Beginning a pickleball program without the use of an organized facility may be a challenge. Approaching the HOA of a subdivision or the city's recreation department with convincing information regarding pickleball and its growth is the place to start. This is an opportunity for an instructor to be a great marketing agent for the game! One should be prepared to give the facts and history of pickleball in a professional but enthusiastic appeal. The hopeful outcome is getting approval for the program from the city or

HOA. Becoming familiar with the policies of the city's recreation department or HOA at this time will prevent any future problems.

If the subdivision or park has tennis courts available, then decisions regarding schedules should be clarified. Specifically, days and times needed for conducting lessons, as well as any court fees that would apply should be discussed. (I found that not enough court time was generated to cause any conflict with the tennis players in my subdivision nor did I need to pay court fees.)

If the subdivision or park has no tennis courts, then the pickleball program director or instructor should ask if the city's recreation department or HOA would be willing to designate a particular area for pickleball courts and to have pickleball lines painted. If the city or HOA is not willing to have the lines painted, then the person in charge could purchase court tape or sidewalk chalk to construct the court.

Having to construct the pickleball court in this way shows one's enthusiasm and a real devotion for the sport, which will reap big benefits for the instructor, as well as for the growth of the sport.

Being aware of other potential players in neighboring subdivisions is also a plus. If other subdivisions are relatively close, then mixers and friendly competitions can be created! (All proceeds will most likely be yours!)

Alex's Story

"Pickleball?? What kind of game is named after something so nondescript? I had never heard of such a game before coming to Hot Springs Village. A paddle—okay, I get that. A net kind of like tennis only different—okay. A court—and it has a kitchen?! And then there is the wiffle ball. That's how I first heard about the game. It sounded bizarre, but I had to try it!

My wife, Cindy, and I decided to give it a whirl after our neighbor told us about this crazy game. Our friends told us they played at a local church that had three indoor courts; so we decided to check it out. We played, were immediately hooked, and went back the next day to play some more. By day three we had bought paddles and decided that we had found our new game. We couldn't get enough!

While we enjoyed the indoor play (since conditions were always the same), we wondered about playing outdoors with the introduction of the sun, the wind, and the temperature variables. We knew there were some outdoor courts but they were 12 miles away. We were cautious about joining the pickleball club in case outdoor play wasn't our thing.

After some consideration, I decided that we could make our own court in our cul-de-sac. Traffic was limited other than the daily visit from the mail lady. The plan came together. I made the net from some screening that I had saved from a backyard gazebo project, along with some spare PVC pipe. A quick run to the local hardware store for the PVC connectors and we were in business! We put a net together that would span the street and marked out the court lines with chalk. It was GAME ON in the hood! And my version of "Barrio Ball" (or "PB in the Barrio" as we call it), was begun! "

Organizing program details and preparing lesson plans in advance will guarantee success even in an independent program. Some details to consider are:
- Preparing a biography with included photograph to be sent to the neighborhood newspaper to introduce the director or instructor, as well as the game of pickleball. By not publishing instructor lesson rates, the announcement would likely be considered a news release and not an advertisement (and therefore, free).

- Announcing the starting of pickleball in the area by writing articles for the local online neighborhood Google group or newspaper that is sent out to everyone in the subdivision.
- Creating and laminating a sign (protected from the rain) providing pickleball Open Play times and the instructor's name and email address. A bright, colorful sign should be placed in a prominent position such as a main column, pole, or the gate of the tennis courts.
- Publicizing a free introductory clinic on a Saturday for adults and also one for kids. To increase enthusiasm and fun, have players bring their own food and beverages for tailgating together after the event. The kids could bring their super soaker water guns to keep cool if the event is scheduled during the summer months!
- Making and posting a sign-up list for players interested in lessons. This should include dates for Open Pickleball, at which time they could practice their skills after the free introductory event. Using the sign-up information, contact the players and form a lesson group (or two, or more!).
- Naming kids' groups to excite interest. Create names such as *Future Stars* for kids 6 to 8 years old, *Shooting Stars* for those aged 9 to 11, and *Rising Stars* for 12 to 14 year olds. Other fun names could include *Top Siders*, *Spinners*, or *Sweet Pickles*. (Just have fun with it!)
- Considering the time needs of any adult groups. Schedule group lessons for moms during the day when their children are in school and for working men on Saturday mornings. (You're the boss—be creative and flexible!)
- Celebrating the launch of the pickleball program by scheduling a Family Night with each family bringing peanut butter and jelly sandwiches

Lesson Plans—Who Me?

Planning and writing lessons for the different skill groups and finding enough drills and games for one hour of lesson time each week for six weeks can be a challenge for a beginning instructor. With determination and patience it can become much easier. See Appendix I for an example of a beginner lesson plan.

When I began teaching tennis years ago, I was quite inexperienced but with a heart for teaching. I searched the Internet for examples of drills and adapted my own to fit my group of players. I also discovered that teaching kids is much easier than teaching adults because the kids have a tendency to accept adult authority and never question anything. They just want to have fun and learn something new.

It takes an enthusiastic instructor to keep kids interested and wanting more. Adults can be critical and may question an instructor's ability to teach them a skill they believe they already have. On the other hand, adults can also be very affirming and encouraging. Facial expressions and body language are a dead giveaway that a person is either enjoying the lesson or thinks it is "the pits." A drill or game may have to be sacrificed to keep players engaged.

Lesson plans might need to be adjusted for different instructors and groups. For example: If an advanced group of players is being taught the rudiments of pickleball instead of skills and patterns of play that will fit their skill level, then the instructor is not meeting their needs. If an instructor motivates and challenges players with skills appropriate to the group, the instructor will continue to have players who stay engaged and continue to come back for more lessons. The keys to a great lesson are teaching well-prepared drills, keeping the players active and moving, and allowing the players to apply their skills by playing in a match situation.

Preparing lessons for any group should begin with a written list of drills that could be taught for six weeks. Drills may be divided by their importance with court diagrams placed beside them for each week.

When meeting the group for a scheduled lesson, it is very helpful to attach the lesson plan to a small clipboard or electronic tablet (such as an iPad) for review before beginning and during a lesson. (Just don't forget the tablet or clipboard!)

Recording player feedback next to the drill can be a great aid in deciding if a skill is worth keeping or throwing out. It also gives an instructor insight on how to become better at planning lessons, as well as how to improve his or her teaching methods. I know I always appreciated feedback. A few times I thought a drill was really great but then scrapped it during the lesson because nobody could execute the drill or it was just plain dull! We learn by doing!

Create Additional Revenue—Increase The Yield

A hosting facility for a new pickleball program will be interested in the possibility of future revenue growth. Being able to project future growth with facts and figures at the initial meeting will greatly enhance the prospects of being approved for the program.

When I began developing a pickleball program at the Cypress Creek YMCA in Houston, I began with only six players on one court. Because all six players were beginners, I proposed that if the YMCA hired me as a paid instructor, then I would do my best to build a lasting pickleball community that would result in increased revenue for their facility. During the next several years, the YMCA hired two additional instructors who helped teach beginner and intermediate lessons. Four courts were added that allowed pickleball players more court time. The end result was increased memberships and, therefore, increased income for the facility.

Examples of detailed actions for increasing income included:

- New beginning players desiring to join the pickleball program were required to pay for six weeks of lessons before being allowed to participate in Open Play, unless they were already experienced tennis players. Beginner lessons, offered every six weeks, were always filled. This occurred because word spread that a passionate instructor would be teaching them. (For this reason, beginner classes were full. Attitude makes all the difference!) I never remember losing a new player because they did not want to take a set of lessons.
- Additional classes were formed (and paid for) as players advanced in skill level. Advanced Beginner, Intermediate, and Advanced lesson groups formed as a result of the first group of beginners I began teaching in 2008. After one year of lessons, these beginners were all playing tournaments and winning medals!

- Community and neighboring area events were scheduled. Monthly mixers that included invitations to players from other facilities were organized. Each player paid $10 for the Round-Robin doubles play. Typically, these events drew 25 to 32 players per mixer. The facility offered free food at its own expense but still produced more than enough profit to cover the cost of the food.
- Pickleball tournaments promoted by a facility are great revenue generators. Tournament entrance costs, required guest fees for those who are not members of the facility, and the purchase of food or snacks will reap additional benefits.
- Discounted pricing packages for players taking private or semi-private lessons can be created and may be quite popular.
- If the facility has extra gym time available, then Open Play can be divided up into matches involving all skill levels. This could attract more player memberships if all at various skill levels did not have to play together on a limited number of courts. Although the program will be built with beginners, losing top players because they can't get enough competition with those at their own skill level would not be a good outcome. In all probability, they will be looking for another venue!

Consider The Budget—Count The Cost

Before beginning any program, it's always important to consider the budget, whether working independently or working for a facility. Examples of items to consider and discuss with a facility director are listed below.

Working independently:
- Expense for an umbrella liability insurance policy
- Cost of balls, nets, ball carts, court accessories, demonstration paddles, and other items
- Expenses for items such as office supplies, photocopies, and promotional materials
- Marketing expense

Working for a facility:
- Fees paid for additional instructors
- Cost of lost or damaged balls, nets, or paddles
- Expenses for the use of a facility's office supplies and copy machine
- Food or snacks purchased for socials, events, and mixers
- Member and nonmember lesson rates
- Event entrance fees

Best Pickleball Tips

Start small and build
Plan ahead
Create exciting and out-of-the-ordinary events
Build harmony among the players
Develop a training program
If something doesn't work, then change the times, dates, lessons, instructors
Be passionate, be an entertainer, and have fun!

ONE COURT AT A TIME

Thanks!

I am so excited that you have decided to begin a new adventure with pickleball. As you follow this pickleball plan, I believe it will help you develop the game with both adults and children. As you explore the opportunities around you, people will see not only your passion for the game, but also your joy as they enjoy themselves. You will see a change in their character and the joy of new friendships through the game of pickleball.

You must **VALUE** it, **STAND** behind it,
and be a **CHAMPION** for the pickleball program!

You and those you introduce to the game are *WINNERS!*

Appendix I
Skill Assessment Rating Sheet

2.0 Skill Assessment Rating Sheet

Name:_____ Self-Rating:_____ Date:_____

Email:_____ Cell Phone:_____ #Games Observed:_____

Weather Conditions:_____

To be filled out by the Rating Team:

2.0 SKILL LEVEL—SHOULD ALSO POSSESS MOST/ALL 1.5 SKILLS	0	1	2	3
Knows **some of the basic rules**, "two bounce rule" and scoring				
Demonstrates a **forehand groundstroke**				
Demonstrates a **backhand groundstroke**				
Demonstrates a **volley**				
Demonstrates an **overhead smash**				
Gets some **serves** into the **correct** service square				
Knows where to stand as the serve team and the return team				
Has **good mobility**, moving in a safe and balanced manner*				
Has **good quickness***				
Has **good hand–eye coordination***				

SERVE REQUIREMENT—4 OF 10 (40%)	YES	NO
Service Good		
Service foot faults		

SERVE RETURN REQUIREMENT—4 OF 10 (40%)	YES	NO
GOOD FOREHAND		
Good Backhand		

VOLLEY REQUIREMENT—4 OUT OF 10 (40%)	YES	NO
BACKHAND		
Forehand		
Non-Volley Zone foot faults		

Rater's Sign:_____ Actual Skill Level:_____ Player's Sign:_____

Ledger: *0* = not observed or not able to execute; *1* = attempted but very poorly executed/needs work; *2* = good basic form, but needs work; *3* = solid, consistent performance

Appendix II
Beginner Clinics
~Drills And Games~
1.5 – 2.0 Skill Levels

Lesson # 1
WELCOME
HISTORY OF PICKLEBALL
COURT ETIQUETTE
COURT LINES
WARM-UP

Ground Strokes

Forehand Ground Strokes—Players form two lines behind the baseline at the right and left service courts. Players in both lines are hitting forehand ground strokes. The instructor should stand on the opposite side of the net with the ball basket.

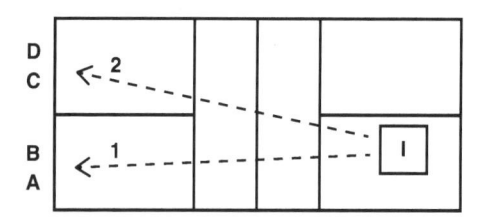

```
   D
   C   <- 2
                              
   B   <- 1           [ 1 ]
   A
```

Or, he or she may want to feed the balls from the same side to be in a better position to access the players to correct grips or strokes. Feed two balls to each player, and alternate feeds from one line to the other to keep the players moving. **Make small adjustments with words or demonstrate the stroke.**

Pick Up the Balls

Backhand Ground Strokes—Players should perform the same drill again but using backhand strokes instead.

Appendix II—Beginner Clinics

Ready Position

Center Stage—Players form one line behind the baseline at the centerline. The first player stands in a ready position for ground strokes. Feed a ball to the forehand side of the player. The player hits the ball and returns to the ready position. The ball is then fed to the backhand side of the player. The player hits the ball and returns to the ready position. After a series of feeds, the player returns to the end of the line. **Encourage Players to change grips after every hit and to use the correct footwork for each stroke.**

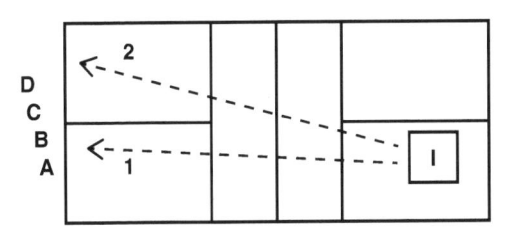

Serves

Serves—Four players may practice serving from the baseline. On the right court, one player serves from near the centerline and the other player serves from near the sideline and vice versa from the left court. So, altogether, four players are serving at the same time. Players rotate from the right court to the left court.

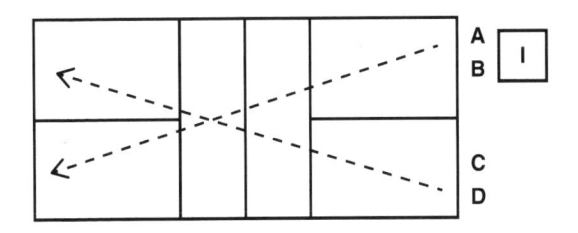

Games

Team Point Singles—Divide the players into two teams. One team stands at one end of the court at the baseline and centerline standing behind each other, with the other team on the other baseline in the same position. Each competitor will be in the ready position. Only one player plays against one player from the other team. Feed balls from the sideline near the net to the forehand side of the player who is to begin the game. The point is played out between both team players. Feed a second ball to the same player's backhand. Play the point out. The next two players compete—one from each team. Continue the game until one team scores 12 points. Players then exchange ends of the court and feed balls to the other team.

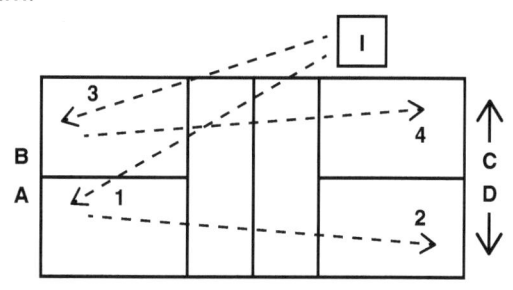

Wrap Up

Answer any questions the players may have about grips and strokes. Pick up the balls, and encourage the players to practice what they learned.

Stroke Notes from Christie

I personally don't teach beginners the rules of the game or show them how to play pickleball until the second lesson unless it is a free introductory class. During the second lesson, I teach and drill ground strokes, volleys, and serves, besides teaching the rules of the game and game play. My *Free Introductory Clinics* are approximately 1 ½ hours in length.

Appendix III
Club or Facility Mixer Flyer Sample

Pickleball Wieners

Can You...
Mustard up the energy?
Relish the game?
BE. THE. WIENER.

Date: Friday March 11
Time: 3:00 – 6:00 pm
Where: Outdoor courts on Desoto Blvd
Format: Open play – choose a court, find someone you don't know or play with friends

HSV Pickleball Club Members ONLY

Hotdogs ★ Sides ★ Appetizers ★ Desserts

★ BYOBeverage & BYOSeating

★ Bring the following based on the first letter of your last name

- A – L ⟶ Desserts
- J – Q ⟶ Side Dishes
- R – Z ⟶ Appetizers

★ Wieners & Condiments will be provided

★ Bring food to the tent near the Rec Building

Menu

Sign up here!
http://www.signupgenius.com/go/20f0f48aeab23a4f49-pickleball1

Come KETCHUP on some good Pickleball fun!

Appendix IV
Out-of-the-Ordinary Mixer Flyer Sample

Vayamos de Fiesta

The salsa is HOT,
the sweat will flow.
It's Vayamos de Fiesta,
ya know!

(SIESTA 🚫)

DETAILS:
Date: Friday May 13
Time: 3:00 – 6:00 pm
Where: Outdoor courts on Desoto Blvd
Format: Open play – choose a court, find someone you don't know or play with friends
HSV Club Members Only

T.O.T.R (Tacos On The Run)

Fiesta Friday

- Taco/salad, Appetizers, Desserts
- BYOBeverage & BYOSeating
- Please bring appetizers like chips, salsa, guac, veggies, dips etc.
- Bring food to the tent near the Rec Building

SIGN UP here:
http://www.signupgenius.com/go/20f0f48aeab23a4f49-vayamos

Appendix V – Demonstration Presentation

Pickleball! That's a crazy name for a racquet sport when you don't even hit a pickle with a paddle. It's actually a "sweet" game for all ages. It's not "dill" at all for those of you who are wondering why you even came to this clinic today. It's better than sumo wrestling! Pickleball can be played anywhere. If you don't have a court near your home, make one in the driveway or set up a net in a cul-de-sac. Invite your neighbors to play or enjoy getting your children involved. Buy four paddles and some outdoor balls or you can even use a broom and two lawn chairs for the net. The court can be made anywhere there is a hard surface. Portable nets can also be purchased from the USA Pickleball Association. There are outdoor facilities, as well as indoor facilities almost anywhere in the country. Just look on *www.USAPA.org* for Places to Play.

~ Presentation Example ~

Pickleball is a combination of ping-pong, badminton, and tennis. If you have played any of these, then you will love pickleball. So, "jar" yourself out of your seat and hit a few balls to join the fun! The sport was created in the summer of 1965 on Bainbridge Island in Washington State when two congressmen decided to create a new game for their bored and restless kids for the summer. Their property had an old concrete badminton court. Since they could not find a set of badminton racquets, they improvised by using ping-pong paddles and a wiffle ball. Although the original game was not named for the family dog, Pickles, it was told later that Pickles would chase the balls and then hide them in the bushes. *Pickleball* became the name of the game in the 1970s when the rules were formalized. Places to play the game began to pop up around the country in fire stations, YMCAs, retirement centers, and elsewhere. Presently, there are over 400,000 players of all ages.

The Strokes

(While two of your famous players are hitting ground strokes at the three-quarter position of the court or while at the baseline hitting easy ground strokes) say something such as "How many of you think this looks pretty easy? So, let's get (a volunteer or someone chosen) to hit eight ground strokes in a row and over the net to win a prize!" (Choose someone who has never played a racquet sport and feed balls high and slow enough so they can hit eight successful forehands over the net.)

(Get the two famous players out on the court again but instruct them not to hit a ball until you give the signal.) Say, "A *volley* is a ball hit into the air, but pickleball players may not hit a volley inside the seven foot area on either side of the net, nor step on the non-volley line while hitting a volley. This area is called *the kitchen*. I guess, boys (speaking to players on the court), you won't be doing any cooking in there!"

"It's show time! Let's see what you can do!" (The famous players then go back and sit down after hitting a few balls.)

Invite a non-racquet sport player to come out and hit a few volleys. "I believe that (volunteer chosen) doesn't play a racquet sport, so let's get him (or her) up here to hit a few volleys. Volleys can be hit with just about anything! I want to show you how easy it is! I am sure your mother taught you while growing up how to make scrambled eggs. Well, we won't be scrambling any eggs in here; that is, unless you step into the kitchen. We want to see how many volleys you can hit with the bottom of the frying pan. Get a good grip on the handle of the frying pan! (Feed about four balls to the volunteer.) Maybe you didn't learn how to scramble eggs but I bet you have taken out the garbage! Let's exchange the frying pan for a garbage can lid! What? You want to try the paddle?" (After he or she hits a designated number of hits, give a prize.)

(Get the famous players back up to serve and return shots.) Say, "Much different than tennis, pickleballs are served underhanded without a bounce. The paddle must be below the wrist at contact. The ball must bounce beyond the non-volley line into the diagonal service box. The *returner* needs to let the ball bounce and the *server*

Appendix V—Demonstration Presentation

needs to let the ball bounce one more time before hitting the ball in the air. (The famous players serve and return several balls as if playing singles). I know you really *relished* the singles match!" (The famous players sit down).

Introduce Drills
I usually introduce volleys, ground strokes, and serves by conducting some short drills just to get players moving and having fun before I introduce them to the game. It's important to explain that players don't need racquet skills to play the game, but then I may choose some skilled players to teach the game without much interruption. Get as many people as possible hitting balls before introducing the game. I found that in my **Free Introductory Pickleball Clinics** people are able to keep a short rally going once they have experienced some success during the drills.

Preview and Play
Explain the actual game if time allows; but if time is limited, just hand out simple rules so the drills and games can begin. (Keep the rules simple.) While conducting doubles play, rotate players in or keep the same four players since the scoring is the most difficult aspect of the game. I give the first servers of each team a red wristband so they can begin to understand scoring and player positioning.

Wrap it Up
Say, "I thank all for coming to the event." (With any other comments; and at the end say) "You might want the autograph of these two famous players!" While in elementary school, my daughter, Charity, was my USA Schools Tennis assistant. She loved the attention from the kids after each tennis assembly.

E-mail Me!

Christie Borne

For families, instructors, facilities, and friends, the Pickleballsisters website is your go-to place for pickleball information. Find us at: *pickleballsisters.com*

If you have any comments send them to *pickleballsisters@gmail.com*.

You can also follow us on
Pickleball Sisters Company Facebook Page